Money; Myth VS Reality

A how-to guide for navigating through financial minefields

CONTENTS

- **Chapter 1**
  Saving ; Myth VS Reality
- **Chapter 2**
  Act of Compounding ; Reality
- **Chapter 3**
  Wealth is freedom ; Reality
- **Chapter 4**
  Luck & Risk ; Reality
- **Putting all together**

Chapter 1

Saving ; Myth VS Reality

Millennials already have a bad reputation for not being frugal. And to a certain extent, it's true.

We all enjoy splurging and partying and think that since we don't know what tomorrow will bring, it's better to spend money today than to save it.

But it's also true that in order to safeguard ourselves against unforeseen costs, we all need emergency savings and to cover our expenses in later life, we all need retirement funds.

There are many financial myths and misconceptions, just like there are with most other topics. For instance, some of us were instructed to save aside at least 10% of each month's pay. Saving money this method wouldn't accomplish much even if you make a moderate salary, because it is useless to hoard cash and stash it away in banks.

Understanding the specifics of money saving and the various variables at play is the sensible thing to do. In that regard, here are five crucial savings myths and their debunking.

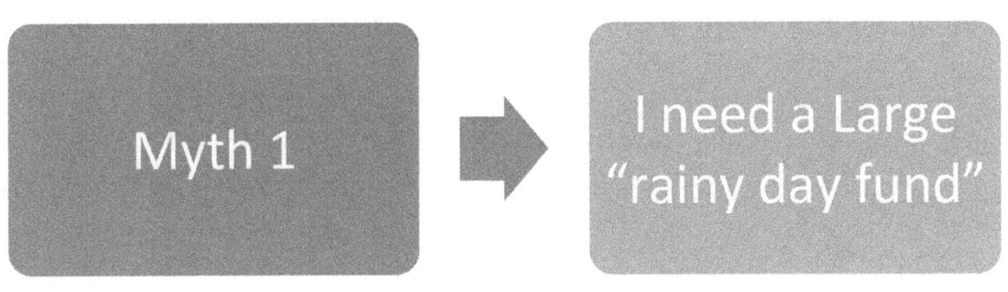

Many will agree that at least of three months' worth of expenses should be saved for crucial expenses, but even a small amount can help with major, unexpected bills and make life a little simpler.

This is false – You can create a meaningful fund even if you can only set aside a little portion of your monthly income. You can still save even if it means reducing your saving quota from your income, because modest amounts saved frequently pile up. (This is the act of compounding which will be discussed in further chapter)

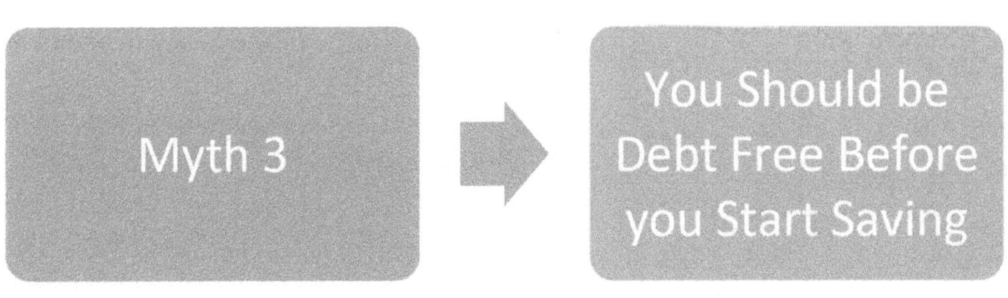

Saving isn't binary – you can both save (as much as you can afford) and reduce debts, a little planning at the beginning of each month will ensure you can save and get your debts down.

First off, there are no predetermined amounts of savings to consider; however, setting up an automated payment to a different account will help. You can save as much or as little as you can afford.

Digital transactions are certainly secured, easier and allows you to keep a record but so long as you set a monthly, affordable level of savings you can always bank a lump sum when required. It is worth noting also that many bank and savings accounts offer cash back and other incentives.

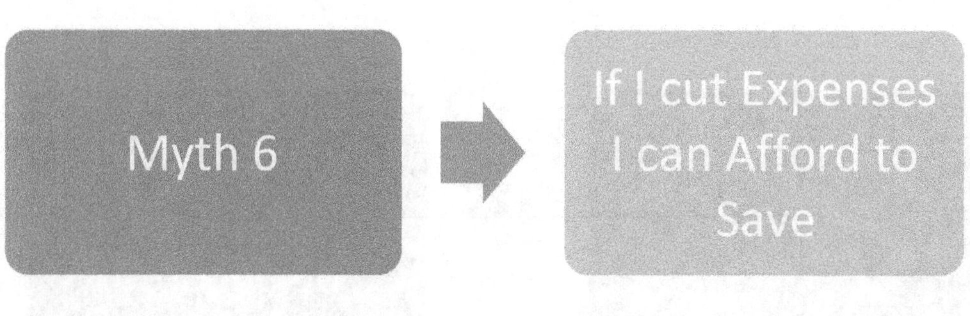

Saving is a strategy – you can cut expenses which may well free up funds to invest but you should stick to your plan – if it means cutting expenses then you can save.

In the current climate it is important to have additional funds to mitigate any unexpected or planned expenditures – the key, however, is having the right strategy that is both affordable and sustainable.

Chapter 2

Act of Compounding ; Reality

Compound interest is actually quite thrilling since it is essentially free money. You're going to turn some heads if you say that out loud. The primary distinction is that compound interest provides free money over time rather than immediately. For young savers who have time on their side, earning interest requires patience, but the payoff can be immensely satisfying.

Think of it this way: Would you prefer to work hard for money or would you prefer to let money work for you? In general, interest on savings accounts allows you to let your money work for you. To help you develop a savings mindset, let's dissect compound interest and explain its what, how, and why.

What is compound interest?

Compound interest is frequently explained using the image of a snowball rolling down a hill. Compound interest is the snow that builds up around your main savings, making it grow larger and larger until your bank account resembles a massive snowman.

And keep in mind that snow has already been added to this snowball without your assistance. Without your intervention, snow (your principle savings) is accumulating more and more as time passes. Not only are your original deposits profitable, but the interest that is collecting (like snow that is piling) is also profitable.

We are constantly trying to "double our money." For whatever reason, whether we're discussing savings accounts, real estate, or the blackjack table, it's an obvious sign of financial success. The Rule of 72 is a simple formula for working out how long it will take to double your money with compound interest at a fixed annual interest rate.

This is how it goes: You can get a rough idea of how many years it will take to double that original investment by dividing 72 by the annual rate of return.

For example

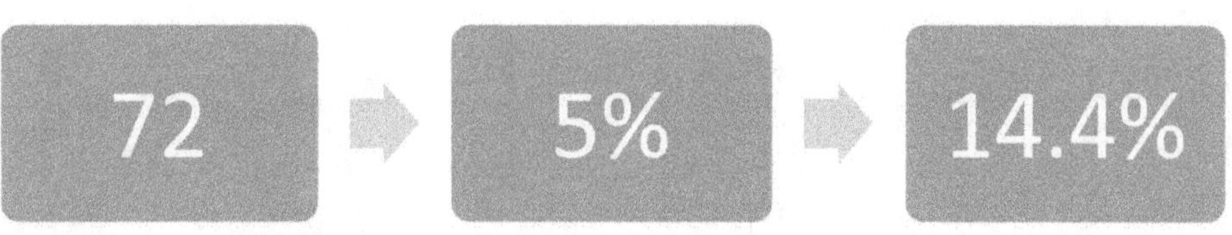

72 divided by a 5% annual interest rate equals 14.4. So, by that equation, it would take over 14 years for a $1,000 savings to become $2,000.

Chapter 3

Wealth is freedom ; Reality

The pursuit of wealth is not the pursuit of material goods. You don't need a $10,000 watch, yachts, sports vehicles, or designer clothing. Those could definitely be entertaining for a while.

The freedom of your time, though, is what genuine prosperity eventually amounts to in the long run. It's the freedom to live your life according to your own schedule and priorities, pursuing the interests and activities that make you happy.

The quest for wealth is the quest for freedom. Build wealth to acquire freedom.

Most wealthy people did not inherit their riches, and most did not become wealthy overnight.

For the majority, it required time, patience, and a little bit of guts. No one of them found it to be simple. Before choosing the proper road, many people presumably tried several others and failed. They all picked up lessons along the way that we can all benefit from.

Here are six hard facts and realities about wealth and freedom:

Freedom Is Not Given.

The ability to use your time anyway you like is not a given and should never be viewed that way. It's not a right, and it's not a path that your employment, your company, or your social position have promised or given you. You won't get it or keep what you already have if you take it for granted. Freedom must be battled for, carefully prepared for, and relentlessly pursued. Our founding fathers did not win our independence by taking shortcuts. Financial freedom cannot be attained half-heartedly.

Boring Investments Are Best.

Put more emphasis on time and less on timing.

Everyone desires instant financial success. For them, timing is everything. Get on the train before everyone else and exit before the price collapses. It's a pointless endeavor. Over time, nobody consistently outperforms the market.

True wealth-building takes time. It takes time to accumulate money using the genuine wealth-building assets, which are the dull ones like commercial real estate, cash-flowing farms, and enterprises. Your wealth will increase over time not only from the compounded income but also from the underlying asset if you take the cash flow from these assets and reinvest it in the same or other cash-flowing assets. You should place more emphasis on time and less on timing because of income and appreciation.

Buy Luxuries With Passive Income And Not Earned Income.

You must discover a means to make money while you sleep if you desire financial independence. The wealthy distinguish themselves from everyone else by focusing their resources and efforts on this passive income.

Because of this, you'll never see them use their salary from their jobs or take out loans to pay for pleasures. They are more drawn to assets with positive cash flow. You won't see them splurge on lovely things for themselves or their families unless they're playing with house money, which is to say, the gains from their investments.

The middle class has no money left over to invest since they spend it all on pleasures. So they keep working until they pass away. The wise investor waits to purchase luxuries until after they have attained their goals and financial freedom

Partnering Is A Must.

You can't attack it on your own. A wise investor will never invest alone. They constantly make use of the time or knowledge of others. Otherwise, they are simply engaging in their usual practice of exchanging time for money. The most savvy investors diversify their portfolios with alternative investments by working with professionals in their respective professions. Why create anything new?

Instead than conquering learning curves and establishing infrastructure to end up dealing with difficulties, wise investors would prefer to spend their time doing what they enjoy. All the obstacles and headaches can be removed by choosing the appropriate partners.

By selecting co-partners with experience and a successful track record, you can invest in asset classes and markets that you otherwise wouldn't consider doing on your own. Through partnerships, you can generate numerous passive income streams from a diversified portfolio that is protected from market downturns. Keep doing what you do best and what you love, and invest with partners who share your passion for the things they do. In this case, everyone benefits.

You Can Fake Rich, But You Can't Fake Wealth.

Influencers and con artists can pretend to be wealthy by renting mansions and expensive cars, but eventually they must pay the pied piper. As a result, they are unable to pay their former investors

(Ponzi), their credit cards are maxed out, and so forth.

Even middle-class people can appear wealthy. They can max out their mansions, automobiles, and credit cards to appear opulent, but they aren't really that rich. Your lifestyle won't change if you lose your work tomorrow, according to true wealth. True wealth can only be produced by assets that produce passive income. True independence cannot be attained with all the designer clothing, pricey automobiles, and extravagant homes in the world.

Real wealth True financial freedom cannot be rushed, manufactured, bought, or obtained with credit cards. It typically originates from resources that other people find unattractive or time-consuming, and it requires patience.

Chapter 4

Luck & Risk ; Reality

Luck and risk are two sides of the same coin. It's impossible to grasp one without understanding the other.

Risk is often described in terms of debatable judgments that might produce undesirable outcomes. Meanwhile, luck is when dubious choices produce favorable outcomes..

We can't control every aspect of our outcomes with our actions, which is why we have the ideas of risk and luck. The effects of other people's decisions can have a much bigger impact on us than our own in a world with approximately eight billion individuals.

Risk makes us realize that some things are beyond our control. Our decision-making is influenced by this information so that we can make the necessary corrections. Having luck has the opposite effect: it deceives us into believing we are in control, which is harmful.

Understanding and controlling risk are crucial when it comes to investing. Luck can't be the same, obviously. You've never heard of a luck consultant because of this. Financial reports are not required to mention lucky breaks. It's an unfair comparison.

We ignore serendipity because our brains are designed to spot patterns in what works. An alluring narrative is the possibility of discovering a method that can be repeated for future rewards. Luck boosts our ego and clarifies confusion.

A good investor should consider luck in addition to risk. For instance, VCs operate on the premise that around 50% of all investments will fail. You'll be better prepared to deal with uncertainty if you take into account the role of luck (success that is not structurally repeatable).

When things are going well, people tend to discount both the risk and the element of luck. The distinction is that it is immediately obvious what went wrong when risk ends your winning streak. It takes us a lot longer to realize the significance of chance.

Even when the outcome is only to clarify reality and lead you to make better decisions, risk might undermine your trust in your judgment. Without enhancing talent, luck can raise confidence, which starts a vicious cycle in which we dismiss luck's part and leave no space for error.

Knowing about risk and luck gives you the ability to accept that there are some things you cannot control. This gives you more time to concentrate on the few things you can manage. You can't avoid danger and luck; you can either learn to manage them or decide to disregard them.

Putting all together

We all have the ability to choose and find meaning in the life that has been given to us by a higher force here on earth. This is where balancing plays a significant part. The first step to financial freedom in wealth building is patience, strategic long-term planning, and goals. Access to knowledge and acting on that knowledge are additional factors. All of the steps provided in this how-to guide are tried-and-true methods that have helped over 100+ people establish their financial footing. These are seminar materials that I made into a book to encourage more individuals to pursue financial literacy.

www.ingramcontent.com/pod-product-compliance
Lightning Source LLC
LaVergne TN
LVHW020545160826
845677LV00015B/4211

* 9 7 9 8 3 5 9 0 8 2 1 6 7 *